Bright
≡Summaries.com

The Words

by Jean-Paul Sartre

BOOK ANALYSIS

Written by Ophélie Ruch
Translated by Emma Hanna

The Words

BY JEAN-PAUL SARTRE

Bright
≡Summaries.com

JEAN-PAUL SARTRE

FRENCH WRITER AND INTELLECTUAL

- **Born in Paris in 1905.**
- **Died in Paris in 1980.**
- **Notable works:**
  - *Nausea* (1938), novel
  - *No Exit* (1944), play
  - *Existentialism and Humanism* (1946), philosophical essay

Jean-Paul Sartre was a French writer and one of the most influential philosophers of the 20th century. His existentialist philosophy attracted both renown and censure, and he authored a great number of essays, including *Being and Nothingness* (1943) and *Existentialism and Humanism* (1946). He also wrote several literary works, including *Nausea* (novel published in 1938), *The Flies* (play written in 1943) and *No Exit* (play written in 1944), which he used to expound upon his philosophical beliefs and his own definition of literature. In 1964, he turned down the Nobel Prize in Literature and published *The Words*, an autobiography focusing on his youth. In addition to his literary output, Sartre was also known for his long-term relationship with Simone de Beauvoir (French writer and philosopher, 1908-1986) and for his far-left political activism.

THE WORDS

THE TALE OF A VOCATION

- **Genre:** autobiographical novel
- **Reference edition:** Sartre, J.-P. (1964) *The Words*. Trans. Frechtman, B. New York: George Braziller.
- **1st edition:** 1964
- **Themes:** literature, writing, deception, identity, childhood, vocation

The Words is Jean-Paul Sartre's autobiography, and was the last literary work he published during his lifetime, first appearing in 1964. It is a faithful account of his childhood from the ages of 4 to 11, and features many of the themes that are typically associated with this genre, including his relationship with his parents, his formative experiences and his gradual self-discovery. The book is divided into two sections of similar length, titled "Reading" and "Writing", respectively. It is structured around Sartre's relationship with words, and initially focuses on his discovery of reading, then his first attempts at writing. This allows him to explore the extent to which his vocation as a writer was the logical result of his personal experiences as a child.

The story of Sartre's childhood provides tremendous insight into the rest of his life and works. It acts as both an explanation and a conclusion, and is a key element of Sartre's extensive literary and critical output.

SUMMARY

The Words is divided into two sections titled Reading and Writing. Aside from this single division, the book takes the form of a continuous text without chapters or sub-sections. It is an autobiographical work which is narrated by the author himself, and it tells the story of his childhood in Paris in a family from the Alsatian industrial middle class.

A SENTINEL OF CULTURE

Sartre's father died when he was very young, leaving him to be raised by his mother, Anne-Marie, and his maternal grandparents, whom he collectively referred to as "Karlémami". This was a portmanteau of his grandfather Karl Schweitzer's given name and his nickname for his grandmother Louise, "Mamie". The young Jean-Paul – or Poulou, as his family called him – therefore grew up surrounded by adults, but without a father figure. As a result, he was granted a certain degree of freedom as a child, and his only duty was to make his guardians happy, which meant trying to become whatever they wanted him to be. For example, they reminded him of the supreme importance of books and reading on a daily basis, which was incomprehensible to him, as he had not yet learned how to read. According to Sartre, this led him to start resorting to pretence, as he was at an age when books were still a source of nothing but mystery for him, but he felt obliged to develop an attachment to them nonetheless. He also describes books as "standing stones" (p. 40) and notes that he was in awe of his grandfather's library, mentioning his fascination with reading and the pristinely ordered shelves on multiple occasions. Books also helped him to find his vocation: to ascend to "priesthood" (p. 67) and become a "sentinel of culture" (*ibid.*) just like his grandfather.

Poulou gradually taught himself to read, all while lying to both the adults around him and to himself on a daily basis. For example, he pretended to read works by great French authors each day, while secretly just reading summaries of their works in the *Larousse* encyclopaedia. However, he also regularly shut himself away in his grandfather's study and forced himself to read the works of classic authors, despite never liking them nearly as much as he enjoyed reading adventure novels. Knowing that his taste in literature diverged significantly from what was considered great fiction, he began ignoring his own preferences in order to fit more closely into the persona he had crafted for himself.

Sartre also describes some of the more elaborate deceptions he tried to pull off as a child because of this narcissism. For example, when a friend of his mother's called Mme. Picard came to visit and gave him a handful of questionnaires, telling him "Fill it in and have your little friends do the same. You will be building happy memories" (p. 107), he decided to try and impress whoever read the questionnaire by making up his answers. However, Mme. Picard immediately saw through his dishonesty, saying, "You know, my dear, it's interesting only if you're sincere" (p. 108).

130 POUNDS OF PAPER

One day, while on holiday with his mother and grandmother, Poulou wrote a poem to his grandfather, who replied with a poem of his own, starting a chain of correspondence in verse between them, which all of the adults found very touching. By the time they returned to Paris, the young Sartre had practically established himself as a writer. He threw himself whole-heartedly into this new pretence, and would ceremoniously settle down at his writing desk just so that everyone nearby could marvel at him, while not actually doing anything more impressive than thinking about the illusion he was projecting. However, the young Sartre's natural fascination with writing developed into something much more profound because of his grandfather's reaction to this behaviour. Karl respected his efforts, but constantly declared that the life of a writer was incredibly difficult, which deepened Sartre's resolve and convinced him to truly dedicate himself to writing. His grandfather therefore played a pivotal role in this decision, as noted by Sartre himself: "he drove me into literature by the care he took to divert me from it" (p. 16).

Writing became a game to him, and he began to love it both because of the enjoyment he derived from it and because of its usefulness. Moreover, it was one of the few hobbies he was able to indulge in: "Being an only child, I could play it by myself" (p. 143). Sartre's story of a habit developed out of necessity could not be further removed from the fanciful tales that more readily spring to mind when we imagine how authors find their calling.

At the age of nine, having accepted his new role as a writer, Sartre was nevertheless assailed by doubts that he could not share with anyone else, particularly about the role of writers and literature. These doubts led to a conversation with the Holy Ghost in a vision (p. 185), which he interpreted to mean that he had been chosen and that he must accept his literary vocation. From that point on, his persona as a writer took on a newly mystical air, and he eventually felt as though he was becoming one with the object of his childhood dreams: "My bones are made of leather and cardboard, my parchment-skinned flesh smells of glue and mushrooms, I sit in state through a hundred thirty pounds of paper, thoroughly at ease" (p. 194).

In this way, Sartre became one with literature as he became a man. He goes into great detail about the ways that this pretence eventually became part of him, and how the people who watched him and read his work gradually created a persona for him that he no longer had any control over, concluding: "I became my own obituary" (p. 206).

NEITHER A WONDER NOR A JELLY-FISH

At the age of ten, the young Sartre started school, where he discovered the joys of friendship. After being shaped into a solitary, narcissistic child by his experiences of a world populated exclusively by adults, he discovered that the real challenge lay in building relationships with children of his own age: "I had met my true judges, my contemporaries, my peers, and their indifference condemned me. I could not get over discovering myself through them: neither a wonder nor a jelly-fish. Just a little shrimp in whom no one was interested" (p. 134).

In this way, he gradually discovered that not only was he an imposter, but he was also not the prodigy that his mother and grandparents had always pretended he was: for example, during one trip to a barber, where his childhood curls were snipped away, his entire family was stupefied to discover that he was an ugly child (pp. 103-104). Everyone's shock was so palpable that it drove him to temporarily abandon his writing.

Tragedy also struck during one particularly cold winter, which led to the death of Sartre's class-mate Bénard. This gave the other children their first taste of grief, as they had respected him and treated him like a kind of mascot. A few weeks later, a new student who resembled Bénard in every possible way joined the class, and even though everyone knew that he was not the same person, it was impossible not to momentarily be-lieve that Bénard had come back from the dead. Sartre approached him during the break, which was the moment the friendship between him and Paul-Yves Nizan (French writer, 1905-1940) was born. In spite of their differing literary and political opinions, this friendship would endure throughout their lifetime.

Despite the traumatic nature of these expe-riences, which shattered many of his childhood illusions, Sartre makes it clear that they also allowed him to mature and develop as an individual.

In fact, all of these early pretences determined the course of the rest of his life, including his career as a writer. This deception was made up of two halves: the false persona that his family built up around him, and the strange relationship with books that Sartre cultivated himself: "My truth, my character, and my name were in the hands of adults. I had learned to see myself through their eyes. I was a child, that monster which they fabricated with their regrets" (p. 83).

He concludes: "Such were my beginnings: I fled; external forces shaped my flight and made me" (p. 248).

CHARACTER STUDY

In any autobiography, the concept of a character is a complex matter, as the protagonist, the narrator and the author of the story are all the same person. Furthermore, the other characters that populate the narrative are not fictional: they really exist, or existed, and are not simply a product of the author's imagination. As such, they do not play a symbolic role in the story in the same way that the characters of a novel do. However, they do still determine the course of the story through their interactions with the protagonist and the ways they shape and influence their fate.

The Words deliberately features a limited number of characters, as the author wanted to emphasise the solitude that defined his early childhood. It is also worth noting that most of these characters are adults, not children, which is a relatively rare occurrence in autobiographical literature.

JEAN-PAUL SARTRE

In accordance with the conventions of auto-biographical literature, the protagonist of this book is the author, Jean-Paul Sartre (nicknamed Poulou by his family).

The book starts when Sartre is 4 years old, and ends when he reaches the age of 11. He is described as a lone child in a sea of adults, whose ego was given the freedom to run wild and who spent his time courting the adults' approval.

He was enthralled by books, and this fascination led him to construct an entire persona which eventually shaped his identity as an adult. The whole story is focused on his personal growth and the formative experiences that influenced it.

KARLÉMAMI

Karl Schweitzer and his wife Louise were Sartre's maternal grandparents. The author often uses a contraction of their names to refer to them both, which reflects the fact that he viewed them as a single entity, and as a kind of substitute for the parental unit he never had. However, their relationship is depicted as somewhat tumultuous, as their beliefs and opinions were often completely at odds.

Louise does not play a particularly significant role in the narrative, echoing the limited role women were expected to play in middle-class families in the early 20th century, whether or not this parallel was deliberate. Conversely, Sartre's grandfather is shown to have been a father to him in all but name: he made decisions for his grandson, encouraged him to pursue his vocation, and inspired both fascination and repulsion in him. Although Sartre says that he was terrorised by his grandfather, Karl also plays a central role in many of the most meaningful passages of the book, which shows that their relationship was certainly as complex as that of a father and son.

ANNE-MARIE

Anne-Marie was Sartre's mother. She was very young when she had her son, and lost her husband shortly after he was born. She then moved back in with her parents, and the young Poulou thought of her almost as an older sister, rather than as his mother: "My mother and I were the same age and were always together" (p. 217). They are very close, particularly because they are both dominated by his grandfather.

Anne-Marie is described as a gentle, patient and loving woman. She played a relatively limited role in her son's upbringing, and only provided him with emotional support, which eventually proved insufficient.

ANALYSIS

AUTOBIOGRAPHY

Autobiography is a relatively new literary genre: the *Confessions* (published between 1782 and 1789) of Jean-Jacques Rosseau (French writer and philosopher, 1712-1778) are generally considered the first published example of an autobiography. An autobiography can be defined as "an account of a person's life written or otherwise recorded by that person" (Collins).

This genre emerged as a result of the rise of individualism, the decline of religion and the evolution of writing conventions, and continued to develop until the 20th century, when it became particularly prevalent. This growing popularity meant that the genre was continuously being subtly redefined with each new autobiographical work that was published, because in spite of the common thread that runs through every auto-biography ever written – namely, its nature as a true account of the author's life, written in the first person – no two autobiographies are entirely alike. On the contrary, each individual work is a reflection of its author and their personal outlook, and is therefore equally unique. In other words, an autobiography is shaped by the way its author views their own life, their commitment to creating an honest narrative, their goal in writing the book, their views on society, their political, philosophical and spiritual convictions, and even their writing style. *The Words* is no exception, as it brings together all of the philosophical and political thought that Sartre developed over the course of his life.

EXISTENTIALISM

In order to understand Sartre's autobiography, it is necessary to have a basic grasp of the philosophy that defined all of his literary output: namely, existentialism. This philosophy, which Sartre developed in the years following the end of the Second World War, became so popular that it could almost be described as fashionable, an epithet that is rarely associated with the field of philosophy.

According to the tenets of existentialism, "existence precedes essence": Sartre did not believe in the existence of human nature, meaning the idea that a person's essence pre-determines their character. Instead, he believed that each individual constructs their own identity, which is defined by their actions. This means that people must act in order to exist, make use of the time they have and fulfil their responsibilities, and also that each individual is entirely free, and therefore wholly responsible for their own actions. This duality of freedom and responsibility formed the basis of Sartre's moral philosophy.

Sartre's existentialist philosophy also influenced his literary works. He believed that producing a work of literature is an action and a way for the writer to engage with the world around them: the author must choose the subject of their work and their target audience, and they are responsible for what they write. This means that all writers are actively engaging with life.

Sartre incorporates a number of his philosophical ideas into *The Words*:

- **Individuals are shaped by their environment**. Sartre was born into a middle-class family, which contributed to his pronounced narcissism, and his career as a writer can be traced back to his grandfather's large collection of books.

- **An individual's identity is shaped by their actions**. For example, the young Sartre's habit of pretending to read and write eventually led to him accepting his vocation as a writer, even though it started as nothing more than a childish game. In this way, Sartre shows that every action has consequences.

- **An individual has a responsibility to live honestly and transparently**. By writing his autobiography, Sartre strips away all semblance of a mask and reveals his true self to the reader.

THE END OF A LITERARY CAREER

By telling the story of his childhood, Sartre removes a metaphorical mask and reveals his true self. He does not attempt to hide the fact that he was born into a middle-class family, nor that he only began writing as a way of impressing others. Similarly, he makes it clear that his relationship with his mother shaped him into a selfish individual and that his ugliness gave him something of a psychological complex, and so on. Furthermore, the act of writing an autobiography is inherently egocentric, which conflicts with Sartre's view that writing should be a means for the author to engage with the era they live in. His decision to write an autobiography illustrates the fact that he is still an egocentric person at heart, in spite of all his theories, and allows him to use writing to lay his own soul bare.

The Words allows Sartre to retrace his own life and denounce the pretences he indulged in. By making these deceptions public knowledge, he is able to deconstruct his own persona as a writer, rendering it unusable. This meant that it would have to be the final act of his literary career, and so he never published any other literary works after *The Words*, only autobiographical and critical works such as the later volumes of his ten-part *Situations* series of essays (published between 1947 and 1976).

FURTHER REFLECTION

SOME QUESTIONS TO THINK ABOUT...

- Analyse the religious metaphor in the passage "I began my life [...] making it creak like a shoe" (pp. 40-41).
- The idea of pretences and facades is one of the book's key themes. To what extent is the author's life shaped by this concept?
- Do you think Sartre's account of his life is completely honest?
- Read one of Sartre's plays, such as *No Exit*, and compare and contrast the philosophical concepts it explores with those explored in *The Words*.
- To what extent are the characters in an autobiography similar to the characters in a novel?
- In your opinion, why did Sartre choose to end the narrative when he started secondary school?

We want to hear from you!
Leave a comment on your online library
and share your favourite books on social media!

FURTHER READING

REFERENCE EDITION

- Sartre, J.-P. (1964) *The Words*. Trans. Frechtman, B. New York: George Braziller.

REFERENCE STUDIES

- Lejeune, P. (1975) *On Autobiography*. Trans. Leary, K. Minneapolis: University of Minnesota Press.

- Sartre, J.-P. (2003) *Being and Nothingness: An Essay on Phenomenological Ontology*. Trans. Barnes. H. E. Abingdon: Routledge.

- Sartre, J.-P. (2001) *What is Literature?* Trans. Frechtman, B. Abingdon: Routledge.

MORE FROM BRIGHTSUMMARIES.COM

- Reading guide – *Dirty Hands* by Jean-Paul Sartre.

- Reading guide – *Existentialism and Humanism* by Jean-Paul Sartre.

- Reading guide – *Nausea* by Jean-Paul Sartre.

- Reading guide – *No Exit* by Jean-Paul Sartre.

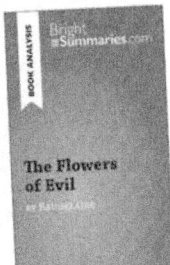

www.brightsummaries.com

Ebook EAN: 9782808010702

Paperback EAN: 9782808010719

Legal Deposit: D/2018/12603/273

Cover: © Primento

Digital conception by Primento, the digital partner of
publishers.

Printed in Great Britain
by Amazon